Greenacres Library
OCT 19 2006

SP J 394 .2646 ZOC
Zocchi, Judith Mazzeo.
On Halloween night = La
noche de halloween /

PALM BEACH COUNTY
LIBRARY SYSTEM
3650 SUMMIT BLVD.
WEST PALM BEACH, FL 33406

written by Judy Zocchi
illustrated by Rebecca Wallis

dingles&company New Jersey

©2005 by Judith Mazzeo Zocchi

All rights reserved. No part of this book may be reproduced in any form without written permission from the publishers, except by a reviewer who may quote brief passages in a review to be printed in a newspaper or magazine.

First printing

PUBLISHED BY dingles&company
P.O. Box 508 • Sea Girt, New Jersey • 08750
WEBSITE: www.dingles.com • E-MAIL: info@dingles.com

Library of Congress Catalog Card No.: 2004092706
ISBN: 1-891997-76-9

Printed in the United States of America

This book is dedicated to Josephine & Mike

ART DIRECTION & DESIGN Barbie Lambert
PHOTOGRAPHY Sara Sagliano
ENGLISH EDITED BY Andrea Curley
SPANISH EDITED BY John Page
ADDITIONAL COPY WRITTEN BY Robert Neal Kanner
EDUCATIONAL CONSULTANTS Kathleen Miller & Anita Tarquinio-Marcocci
ART ASSISTANTS Erin Collity & Sara Sagliano
PRE-PRESS BY Pixel Graphics
SOME ILLUSTRATIONS IN THIS BOOK WERE BASED ON SKETCHES BY Heather Mills

Long ago, people wore scary costumes to fool the evil spirits into thinking they were one of them. Today on Halloween children wear both scary and fun costumes.

On Halloween night you might dress up like a vampire,

La noche de Halloween te podrías disfrazarte como un vampiro,

Hace mucho tiempo, la gente se vestía en disfraces de miedo para engañar a los espíritus malos a pensar que ellos también eran uno de los espíritus. Ahora, durante Halloween los niños llevan ambos disfraces de miedo y de diversión.

Some people think that spirits or souls come back to the world of the living as ghosts. When they appear, they are usually shadowy and semitransparent.

a monster, or a ghost.

un monstruo, o un fantasma.

Alguna gente piensa que los espíritus o almas regresan al mundo de los vivos como fantasmas. Cuando aparecen, usualmente son sombreados y semitransparentes.

Then you ask your friends
which costume
scares them the most!

¡Luego preguntarles a
tus amigos cuál disfraz
los asusta más!

A witch is a woman who practices magic. In folktales, witches are usually ugly.

On Halloween night you might make a witch's brew

La noche de Halloween podrías hacer un brebaje de bruja

Una bruja es una mujer quien ejerce magia. En cuentos populares, las brujas son usualmente feas.

It's a tradition at Halloween celebrations to decorate, play games, and serve food and drinks that represent harvesttime. Halloween party activities may include carving pumpkins, bobbing for apples, and drinking apple cider.

with cinnamon and cider.

con canela y sidra.

Es una tradición en celebraciones de Halloween de decorar, jugar juegos, y servir comida y bebidas que representan la temporada de cosecha. Las actividades de una fiesta de Halloween pueden incluir esculpir calabazas, balancear manzanas con la boca, y beber zumo de manzana.

To scare people,
you can serve it
with a floating fake spider!

¡Para asustar a la gente,
lo sirves con una araña
falsa flotante!

> A haunted house is a spooky residence that is believed to have ghosts and supernatural happenings.

On Halloween night you could visit a haunted house

La noche de Halloween podrías visitar una casa embrujada

> Una casa embrujada es una residencia espeluznante que se cree tener fantasmas y sucesos sobrenaturales

It is commonly believed that a vampire is a dead person who leaves the grave at night and sucks the blood of sleeping persons. Dracula is the most famous vampire in fiction.

to meet Dracula and his wife.

para conocer a Drácula y a su esposa.

Comúnmente se cree que un vampiro es un muerto quien sale de la tumba por la noche y chupa la sangre de personas durmiendo. Drácula es el vampiro más famoso de la ficción.

When they turn into bats
you run for your life!

¡Cuándo se conviertan
en murciélagos que se salve
quien pueda!

Trick-or-treating is a Halloween tradition. Costumed children ring doorbells, shout "Trick-or-treat!" and receive wrapped candy. The phrase means that the children will play a joke if they don't get a treat.

On Halloween night you might go trick-or-treating

La noche de Halloween podrías ir a colectar trucos-o-golosinas

Truco o golosina es una tradición de Halloween. Niños en disfrace tocan el timbre de las puertas, gritan, «¡Truco o golosina!», y reciben caramelos envueltos. La frase significa que los niños harán una broma si no reciben una golosina.

Safety first when trick-or-treating! Carrying a flashlight is wise so that you can see and be seen by others while walking around at night.

with a flashlight and a bag.

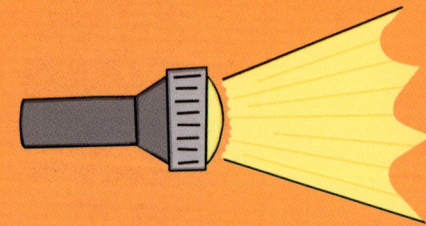

con una linterna y una bolsa.

¡Primeramente, seguridad cuando se va de truco o golosina! Cargando con una linterna es sabio para que puedas ver y ser visto por otros mientras caminando por la noche.

And if you get a lot of candy,
your treat bag will drag!

¡Y si recibes muchas
golosinas, tu bolsa arrastrará!

Halloween is celebrated on October 31. The origin of Halloween goes back to the ancient Celts, who lived in what is today Ireland and Scotland. They held a festival to mark the end of summer and the beginning of harvesttime. The Celts believed that on the night of the feast the spirits of dead people came back looking for a warm fire and a happy time before the long, cold winter began. To celebrate, the Celts lit bonfires, held parades, and dressed in costumes. When Christianity spread to the Celtic lands, the Church set aside the day to remember holy people who had died. The day was called All-hallomas, which means All Saints Day. The night before was called All-Hallows Eve, or All Saints Eve ("eve" is the night before a special day). This name eventually became Halloween!

Halloween se celebra el 31 de octubre. El origen de Halloween viene de los Celtas antiguos, quienes vivían en lo que hoy es Irlanda y Escocia. Tenían un festival que marcaba el fin del verano y el comienzo de la temporada de cosecha. Los Celtas creían que durante la noche del banquete los espíritus de los muertos regresaban buscando un fuego caliente y un tiempo alegre antes que el largo y frío invierno empezara. Para celebrar, los Celtas prendían hogueras, hacían desfiles, y se vestían en disfraces. Cuando Cristiandad llegó a las tierras célticas, la Iglesia apartó el día para recordar a la gente santa quien había muerto. El día se llamó All-hallomas, que significa el Día de todos los santos. La noche antes se llamó All-Hallows Even, o La víspera del día de los santos ("víspera" es el día antes de un día especial). ¡Este nombre con el tiempo llegó a ser Halloween!

DID YOU KNOW...

Use the Holiday Happenings series to expose children to the world around them.

- Pumpkins were once recommended for removing freckles and curing snakebites.
- The largest pumpkin ever grown weighed 1,140 pounds.
- Halloween is second only to Christmas in spending. People will spend more than $2.5 billion during the Halloween season. That's a lot of candy, costumes, decorations, and party goods!
- There is no word that rhymes with orange. Hard to believe for such an important Halloween color.

BUILDING CHARACTER...

Use the Holiday Happenings series to help instill positive character traits in children. This Halloween emphasize Kindness.

- How should you act if you don't like the treat you receive from someone?
- Should you eat any candy while you are trick-or-treating? Why or why not?
- How do you think someone would feel if you made fun of his or her costume?
- How could you help a friend who does not have a costume?

CULTURE CONNECTION...

Use the Holiday Happenings series to expand children's view of other cultures.

- Find out which countries celebrate Halloween.
- How do people in other countries celebrate Halloween?
- Are these celebrations similar to the way you celebrate Halloween?

TRY SOMETHING NEW...

Save some time on Halloween to help hand out treats to others.

For more information on the Holiday Happenings series or to find activities that coordinate with it, explore our website at **www.dingles.com**.

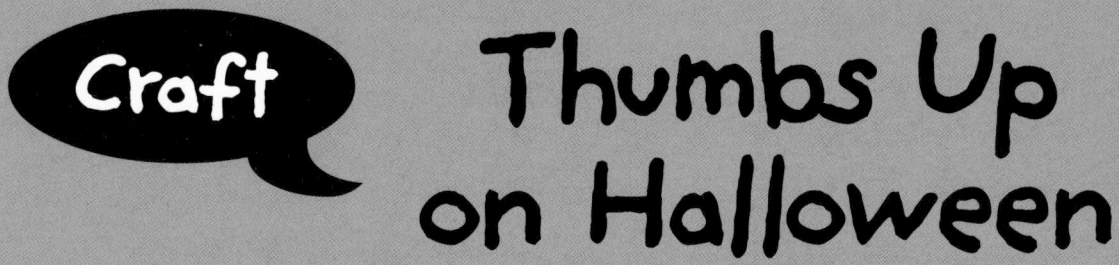

Thumbs Up on Halloween

Goal: To create a Halloween scene

Craft: Create a Halloween scene using thumbprint creatures

Materials:
washable colored stamp pads (or washable paint in a variety of colors and paintbrushes), washable markers, crayons, construction paper, and wipes (to clean your hands)

Directions:
1. Gather materials.
2. Decide what kinds of creatures you want to make out of your thumbprints for your Halloween scene (spiders, witches, ghosts, bats, etc.).
3. For each creature, roll your thumb from side to side in one of the stamp pads and press it on a piece of construction paper.
   (Remember to wipe the ink off your thumb before changing colors.)
4. If you do not have stamp pads, use paint instead. Use a paintbrush to paint your thumb and then roll it on the construction paper.
5. Add eyes, mouths, and other features to your thumbprint creatures with markers and crayons.
6. Create a background for your Halloween scene with markers or crayons.
7. Hang up your picture to decorate your house for Halloween.

To find this craft translated into Spanish bilingual go to **www.dingles.com**.

Judy Zocchi

is the author of the Global Adventures, Holiday Happenings, Click & Squeak's Computer Basics, and Paulie and Sasha series. She is a writer and lyricist who holds a bachelor's degree in fine arts/theater from Mount Saint Mary's College and a master's degree in educational theater from New York University. She lives in Manasquan, New Jersey, with her husband, David.

Rebecca Wallis

was born in Cornwall, England, and has a bachelor's degree in illustration from Falmouth College of Arts. She has illustrated a wide variety of books for children, and she divides her time between Cornwall and London.